MARILYN

A Hollywood Life

MARILYN
A Hollywood Life

ANN LLOYD

BISON GROUP

Page 1: *Marilyn at her most devastating.*

Pages 2-3: *A photograph of Marilyn taken during the filming of* Let's Make Love *(1960).*

Page 5: *The image lingers on – a glamour shot showing the 'public' Marilyn.*

First published in 1989 by
Bison Books Ltd
Kimbolton House
117A Fulham Road
London SW3 6RL

ISBN 0-86124-541-5

Printed in Hong Kong

10 9 8 7 6 5 4 3 2 1

Contents

Left: Early career days as a young model and starlet. Marilyn was a 'natural' in front of the camera. Lenses loved her.

Hometown Story

She was born Norma Jeane Mortensen, to Gladys Pearl Mortensen, at 9.30 am on 1 June 1926 in the Charity Ward of Los Angeles General Hospital. Gladys had previously been married to Jack Baker, by whom she bore Hermitt and Bernice. Jack took his kids with him when he left her in 1923. Her second husband, Edward Mortensen, left her on learning that she was pregnant. Gladys had been having an affair with a man from the film lab where she worked as a negative cutter. Gladys was, therefore, filling Norma Jeane – christened Baker – with movie scenes and movie gossip before she was even born.

After she was born, Gladys didn't feed Norma Jeane with much of anything, for the little girl was farmed out to foster parents while Gladys worked to save for a home – seeing Norma Jeane, when she could, at weekends. It took eight years before she had earned enough for a down-payment on a bungalow and she and her daughter could live together. But only a short while later Gladys was committed to an asylum. There was a strong streak of mental instability in her family; both her parents and her brother lived much of their lives in mental institutions.

Gladys's friend Grace McKee became the little girl's legal guardian; but Norma Jeane remained with various foster parents, plus a spell of nearly two years in an orphanage. It was, all in all, a lonely and unloved childhood. Eventually Grace married a man called Doc Goddard and for the following five years, until she was 15, Norma Jeane had a home.

Then Doc Goddard got a job in West Virginia and Grace decided it was time her ward had a settled life of her own. By now Norma Jeane had curves in all the right places and had attracted the attention of local 19-year-old heartthrob Jim Dougherty. A marriage between the teenagers was arranged. The wedding took place on 19 June 1942.

The couple moved into their own apartment, and Norma Jeane began housekeeping and coping with wartime rationing. Jim joined the Merchant Marines. In due course he was shipped out to the Pacific – leaving behind a bored wife. Even frequent trips to the local movie house and daydreams of becoming a movie star only filled up a bit of the day, so she got a job at a local factory.

It is here that the Marilyn Monroe story really begins. An army photographer had been instructed to take morale-boosting shots of women doing war work. He spotted Norma Jeane – and 26 June 1945 saw her on the cover of *Yank* magazine. With a new-found confidence, she took herself off to Emmeline Snively's Blue Book Modeling Agency.

Norma Jeane, who was getting blonder, now decided that marriage and modeling didn't mix, and Jim reluctantly agreed to a divorce. By 1946 she was on magazine covers everywhere. Miss Snively arranged an appointment with Ben Lyon, the talent scout at Twentieth Century-Fox film studio, who gave her a screen test. The verdict was that she had that essential starlet attribute known as 'flesh impact,' and Lyon was ordered by studio boss Darryl Zanuck to sign her up. Lyon's next significant act was to give the new girl a new name. He decided on Marilyn, after stage-musical star Marilyn Miller, and Norma Jeane suggested 'Monroe,' after her maternal grandmother. And so Marilyn Monroe was born.

Marilyn was, however, only the newest in a long line of beautiful girls known as 'the Fox blondes.' Her first walk-on part was in *The Shocking Miss Pilgrim* (1947). She can next be glimpsed in the distance in *Scudda Hoo! Scudda Hay!* (1948), followed by an enormous jump to the role of Eve, a waitress who had three whole lines in *Dangerous Years* (released in 1947).

But from 26 August 1946 when Fox signed her first contract, for a whole year, Marilyn reported to the studio each morning. She attended classes in voice production, drama and movement, and spent the rest of the day being available to the studio photographers for 'cheesecake' pictures, and doing statutory starlet jobs such as opening supermarkets. Also, at this time, Marilyn caught the eye of studio mogul Joe Schenck. Whatever transpired, it didn't inspire Schenck to promote Marilyn's career at Fox, or to intercede when Fox dropped her contract in August 1947.

Then suddenly Joe Schenck 'came good' and arranged for her to test at Columbia Studios. They put her under contract and into *Ladies Of The Chorus* (1943). She had two songs, looked gorgeous, and got her first (favorable) review. Columbia weren't convinced and dropped her, but while at the studio she met several people who were to have a big impact on her life. One was Fred Karger, a musician who did vocal coaching, with whom she fell deeply in love but who wouldn't marry her. Another was Natasha Lytess, Columbia's head drama coach, who saw great promise in Marilyn and invited the young actress to move in with her. However, months of modeling were to follow before another film role would appear.

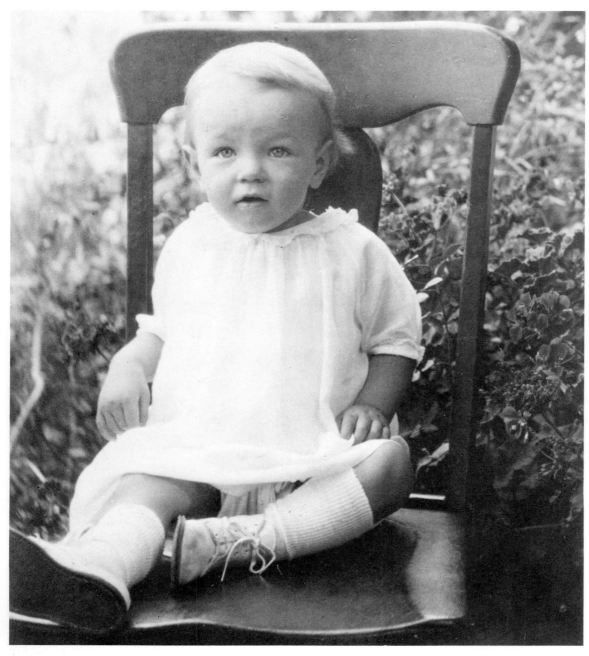

Right: *All the sweetness and sparkle of Marilyn is already here in this lovely child. But so, too, are the seeds of uncertainty, of loneliness and fear of abandonment. Norma Jeane had already lived with several different foster families before her mother was first taken to a mental hospital. At that point the little girl became the legal ward of Grace McKee, Gladys's best friend. Grace could not keep the child herself, and placed her in the Los Angeles Orphans Home in 1935. When Gladys got married – to a man called Doc Goddard, with three children from his previous marriage – she did take Norma Jeane out of the Home. However, it was Grace's Aunt Ana Lower whom Norma Jeane dearly loved, and lived with whenever she could.*

Above: *Marilyn Monroe started a step ahead of most movie stars, for she was born on Hollywood's doorstep. It's not clear who her father was. When Gladys gave birth to Norma Jeane at 9.30 am on 1 June 1926 in the Charity Ward of Los Angeles General Hospital, she had recently been abandoned by husband number two, Edward Mortensen. He may well have left because he suspected her of having an affair with Stanley C Gifford, a man employed by Consolidated Film Industries where Gladys worked as a film cutter.*

Right: *When she was only two weeks old, Norma Jeane was despatched to her first foster home; Gladys didn't feel able to raise her daughter on her own. She did, however, usually go to visit the child on Saturdays. By the time Norma Jeane was eight, Gladys had saved enough for the down-payment on a bungalow. She and Norma Jeane moved into two of the rooms – and rented out the rest. Unfortunately, this togetherness only lasted for a few months; then Gladys had a mental breakdown and was taken back to Los Angeles General Hospital.*

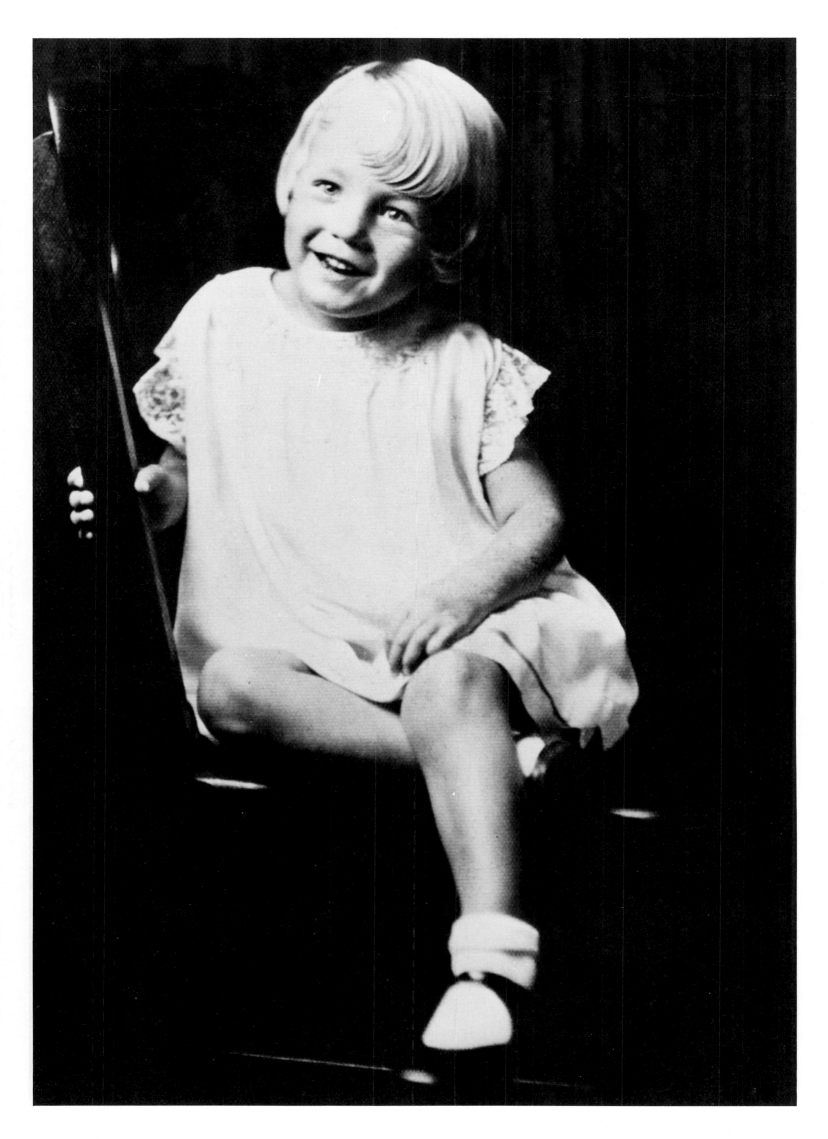

Left: *So delighted was André de Dienes with his first photographs of Norma Jeane that he persuaded her to go away with him on a photographic safari. The trip took them to Las Vegas and the Mojave desert and then on to Portland, Oregon, where he met Norma Jeane's mother. André noted that 'The reunion between mother and daughter lacked warmth. They had nothing to say to each other.' André decided that he and Norma Jeane should be married. He returned to New York to settle his affairs, but when he phoned Norma Jeane to ask if she had finalized her divorce from Dougherty he was to hear: 'But André, I don't want to get married . . . I want to get into movies.'*

Above: *An ecstatic smile from the new Miss Marilyn Monroe. On 19 July 1946 Ben Lyon, talent scout for Twentieth Century-Fox, had given her a screen test. As a result, Fox signed her first contract. Lyon decided Norma Jeane needed a new name; he picked Marilyn, she picked Monroe – after her maternal grandmother. Marilyn then decided to get divorced. As she explained to Jim, who was still away at sea, it was essential to her career that she be single.*

Left: *Two-year-old Norma Jeane out for the day with her mother. Gladys had a frightening family history of mental illness. Both her own parents and her brother spent long stretches in mental institutions. In 1945 Gladys left hospital, and she and Norma Jeane set up home again for about seven months. Marilyn was later able to pay for her mother to stay in a comfortable nursing home when Gladys felt unable to cope on her own. Gladys became more and more involved with religion as the years went by. She died of a heart attack in 1984.*

Right: *Norma Jeane (sixth row from top, fourth from left) in 10th grade – aged 15. She abandoned her education at this stage in order to marry handsome neighbor Jim Dougherty. Grace and Doc Goddard were set to leave California, and Grace was keen to see her ward settled before she left. In 1951 Marilyn returned to college to do a Background to Literature course at UCLA. However, the publicity hounds who pursued her constantly made it impossible for her to study.*

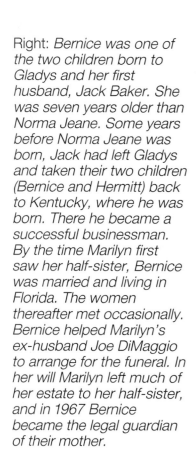

Right: *Bernice was one of the two children born to Gladys and her first husband, Jack Baker. She was seven years older than Norma Jeane. Some years before Norma Jeane was born, Jack had left Gladys and taken their two children (Bernice and Hermitt) back to Kentucky, where he was born. There he became a successful businessman. By the time Marilyn first saw her half-sister, Bernice was married and living in Florida. The women thereafter met occasionally. Bernice helped Marilyn's ex-husband Joe DiMaggio to arrange for the funeral. In her will Marilyn left much of her estate to her half-sister, and in 1967 Bernice became the legal guardian of their mother.*

Above: *André de Dienes was quick to observe the beautiful quality of Norma Jeane's skin, 'smooth, polished, the type which reflects light instead of absorbing it.' He remembers that she came to him a sweater-and-skirt girl, and that he bought her first pair of jeans. Even in this early picture, with her hair tied roughly back, with chipped nail varnish and with her waist-high white knickers sticking up over her jeans, she still has a very special magic.*

Right: *Norma Jeane didn't work with de Dienes again. The next time they met she was Marilyn Monroe. It was the summer of 1949 and she was in New York doing a promotional tour for the Marx Brothers film* Love Happy *in which she had a tiny role. André rushed out and bought two swimsuits, two parasols and 'Knowing my favorite model's appetite, I also prepared a lavish picnic.' They set off for Tobey Beach, about 80 miles from New York, and spent the whole day making wonderful pictures.*

Above: *Norma Jeane became Mrs Jim Dougherty on 19 June 1942 – just after her sixteenth birthday. They moved into their own apartment and Jim returned to his job at Lockheed Aviation. But it was wartime, and Jim wanted to be in uniform, so he joined the Merchant Marines. At first he was based on Catalina Island, and she stayed there with him. Then, at his request (he wanted to see some action), he was shipped out to Australia. Norma Jeane moved in with his parents, and spent her time writing letters to Jim or day-dreaming at the movies.*

Right: *The way men looked at his wife when she was wearing one of her sweaters always made Jim very angry. After he went to sea, a bored and lonely Norma Jeane took a job at the local Radio Plane company. She was spotted by David Conover, an army photographer who was there to take photos of women doing essential work for the war effort. He snapped her in her overalls, then asked if she had a sweater with her – and took some more shots after she had finished work. One of these appeared on the cover of* Yank *magazine.*

Left: *Encouraged by the success of her first published photograph, Norma Jeane took herself off to the Blue Book Modeling Agency. Its head, Miss Emmeline Snively, signed up Norma Jeane on condition that she enrol for a modeling course – which she could pay for out of her first modeling fees. Miss Snively was impressed with Norma Jeane; she taught her how to improve her smile, and persuaded her to straighten and then lighten her hair. Miss Snively remembers that 'She looked a fright at first but, my, how she worked.' It was Emmeline who put Norma Jeane in touch with the agents who fixed up her first interview with Twentieth Century-Fox. She also introduced her new model to famous photographers. One of the first to fall under her spell was André de Dienes, who, in December 1945, took this picture of the girl he fell in love with.*

Left: *When he first met her in 1945, André de Dienes said to Marilyn, 'You will become the world's most photographed beauty; and when I will be old I shall write stories about women, and you . . .' In 1986, the year after his death, de Dienes's book* Marilyn Mon Amour *was published. It contains some of the most beautiful sequences of pictures of Marilyn that have ever been taken – including this one from their 1949 session at Tobey Beach.*

Above: *The young Marilyn was much sought after by the studio publicity boys. But lovely though she was even then, the face that would before long be known far and wide is hardly yet visible. She's still smiling naturally – showing too many teeth and leaving the upper lip short. Her nose has yet to be trimmed; her chin has still to be made firmly rounded; her top front teeth will be slightly straightened – and her hair will 'grow' softer and blonder.*

Above: *Marilyn, it seems, wasn't averse to exercise, although not much interested in sport. There are very early pictures of her jogging – long before it was fashionable. She has been pronounced 'way ahead of her time when it came to female bodybuilding.' Norma Jeane apparently began weightlifting in 1943, and information on her 'starlet training' from 1951 reveals that she regularly did 40 minutes of calisthenics plus a workout with two five-pound dumbbells.*

Right: *A bust that had to be kept in shape. Though Marilyn never wore a bra (or panties) under her slinky dresses, reasoning that they would spoil the line, there are reports that she wore a bra at night – which she put on immediately after making love. Marilyn's bust-waist-hip statistics seem to have been a constant variable. The Blue Book Modeling Agency gave them as 36-24-36. Fox in the early Fifties had them down as 36½-23-34. On being asked by a reporter whether she wore falsies, Marilyn replied 'Those who know me better, know better.'*

Right: *Posing for shots to publicize the Fox Studio Club annual golf tournament – but Marilyn still hadn't made a movie, in spite of having been on contract for over nine months. The studio's publicity had announced in December 1946: 'To date, Marilyn has no picture assignments; she's down for six months of intensive grooming before she faces a camera, with dramatic lessons, dancing lessons, and voice training.' In fact Marilyn was in front of a camera almost constantly; few days would go by without her posing for some publicity shot that needed a willing young blonde.*

Left: *Photographer Philippe Halsman first met Marilyn while shooting her with these other Fox trainee starlets. He has said, 'I remember that one of the girls was an artificial blonde by the name of Marilyn Monroe, and that she was not one of the girls who impressed me the most.' They would meet again.*

Sincerely Marilyn Monroe

Left: *Another publicity shot – but Marilyn had also started to appear in films. Reliable reference sources now state that she was cast in* The Shocking Miss Pilgrim *(1947), starring Betty Grable, but it's unclear whether or not she made it through to the final print. However, she certainly was in* Scudda Hoo! Scudda Hay! *released in 1948, and can be glimpsed, in the distance, in Technicolor, with another girl in a canoe. Sadly, her first line of dialogue – 'Hi' – was left on the cutting-room floor.*

Above: *Posing as 'Miss Cheesecake' for Michael's Cheesecake Bakery. She was also voted 'Cheesecake Queen' by* Stars and Stripes, *'The Present All GIs Would Like to Find in Their Christmas Stocking,' 'The Girl Most Wanted to Examine' by the 7th Division Medical Corps, and 'The Girl Most Likely To Thaw Alaska.'*

Below: *Fox were finding plenty of publicity work for their new blonde, but not much in the way of movies. Of those early, uncertain years she was to say: 'When you're a failure in Hollywood, that's like starving to death outside a banquet hall, with smells of filet mignon driving you crazy.'*

26

Left: *An especially lovely studio portrait – and then another tiny film role, this time as a waitress called Eve who works in a jukebox joint where the town's troubled youth hangs out in* Dangerous Years. *It was a career leap, no less, for it gave her a close-up and three lines of dialogue. However, at this point in a plainly promising career, the studio decided not to renew her contract.*

Above: *At the time Fox dropped her, photographer Bill Burnside was a friend (and probably lover) she could lean on. She inscribed this photo 'Anything worth having is worth waiting for!'*

Right: *A dreadful publicity shot for* Ladies Of The Chorus, *a job which Marilyn's 'close friend' Joe Schenck of Fox was able to arrange with fellow mogul Harry Cohn of Columbia. Marilyn positively glowed in the film. She had two songs, 'Everybody Needs A Da Da Daddy' and 'Anyone Can Tell I Love You,' and these attracted her first review. But Columbia let her contract lapse.*

Left: *An evocative image of Marilyn. This publicity shot was taken in 1952, the year she finished her first screen drama,* Clash By Night, *and the year of the nude-calendar story.*

The Blonde Gentlemen Prefer

Groucho Marx was the man who next came to Marilyn's rescue. He needed a walk-on blonde for the new Marx Brothers comedy *Love Happy* (1950). A long gap followed. It was at this moment that she was asked to pose for some nude-calendar photographs. Marilyn had always said 'no' to nudes – thinking they would hurt her career; but now the prospect of a $50 fee was too enticing.

Love Happy had, however, brought her to the attention of Johnny Hyde of the powerful William Morris Agency. He began using the agency's connections to launch Marilyn's career. Furthermore, Johnny Hyde fell head-over-heels in love. He wanted desperately to marry her and provide for her future (he was a rich man with only a short time to live), but Marilyn said she couldn't; she loved him dearly but she wasn't in love with him. After he died in December 1950 she had to be rescued from a suicide attempt.

Professionally, 1950 was a good year for Marilyn. Hyde had negotiated for her the role of Angela, beautiful blonde 'niece' to a wealthy crooked lawyer in *The Asphalt Jungle*. The public started to notice her. Her next noticeable role was as Miss Caswell, an aspiring starlet in *All About Eve* (1950), and Fox were impressed enough to sign her to a new (and better) contract. However the following year offered her nothing more than blonde-cutie roles.

Her first drama was *Clash By Night* (1952). As filming finished the press announced that they believed Marilyn to be the model in a nude-calendar story. The studio instructed her to deny everything, but Marilyn decided to come clean – she had needed the money. The public forgave her, and the 'Golden Dreams' calendar rapidly became a collectors' item.

In April, *Life* magazine featured her on their cover and called her 'the talk of Hollywood . . . the most talked-about actress in America.' Then it was secretary time again – this one couldn't even type – in *Monkey Business*. It was this film that occasioned her meeting with America's best-loved baseball hero, Joe DiMaggio, on a blind date. They had dinner again the next night, and the next, and the next . . .

There followed further revelations about her past. Studio publicity had always stated that she was an orphan, but a media hound discovered her mother in a mental home. Again Marilyn came through, explaining that her close friends knew her mother was alive and that 'since I have become grown and able to help her, I have contacted her.'

Her next big role was in *Niagara* (1953) as a sizzling *femme fatale* who persuades her lover to murder her husband. *Niagara* was a winner – a fact reflected by Marilyn's receiving the *Redbook* Award for Best Young Box Office Personality. She now moved into a role that could have been tailor-made for her – Lorelei Lee in *Gentlemen Prefer Blondes* (1953). Marilyn's performance helped secure her *Photoplay*'s Best Actress Award the following year, and won for both her and co-star Jane Russell the accolade of being asked to add their hand and footprints to Grauman's Chinese Theater's hall of fame. *Photoplay* had already honored Marilyn as the Fastest Rising Star of 1952.

In *How To Marry A Millionaire* (1953) Marilyn starred alongside Lauren Bacall and Betty Grable. After only a couple more films Grable would retire as Fox's No. 1 Blonde, and leave Marilyn to step into her shoes (and her dressing room). Her role in this film enabled Marilyn to prove that she could look gorgeous in glasses, while the next, *River Of No Return* (1954), had her looking just as good in jeans.

In August 1953 Marilyn had a photo session with fashion photographer Milton Greene. They struck up an immediate rapport. She told him that she still had no control over the sort of movies she made. Indeed, a few months later the studio suspended her for refusing to make *The Girl In Pink Tights*. Greene was convinced that he could help her gain professional independence.

On 14 January 1954, after keeping the world waiting for two years, Marilyn finally became Mrs Joe DiMaggio. In February Marilyn and Joe gave themselves a honeymoon in Japan. On their arrival Marilyn was approached by the US Army which wanted to fly her to Korea to entertain the troops there. She later described the occasion as one of the happiest of her life.

The next film to do Marilyn any justice was *The Seven Year Itch* (1955). She's not an on-the-make blonde in this one, she's 'The Girl Upstairs' – who happens to be an innocently sensuous blonde bombshell, and just the thing to activate summer bachelor Tom Ewell's seven year itch. This was the film with the famous 'skirt scene.' Over 1000 New Yorkers watched happily as Billy Wilder ordered take after take of Marilyn's skirts blowing over her head. Unfortunately Joe DiMaggio was watching too. Marilyn and he had been quarreling more and more often about her film roles and her public 'performances,' and he never recovered from this one. The following month the DiMaggios announced their divorce.

Above: *After* Love Happy *Fox gave her a one-off bit part in* A Ticket To Tomahawk *(1950). She played a very decorative showgirl called Clara, and performed 'Oh, What A Forward Young Man You Are' with three other showgirls and the film's star – Dan Dailey.*

Right: *Months of modeling followed Columbia's axing. Then a tiny walk-on role came up for the Marx Brothers'* Love Happy *(1950). She had to walk in such a way that when she came to detective Groucho and said 'Some men are following me,' he would waggle his famous eyebrows and say 'I can't imagine why!' She easily got the part.*

Below: *Johnny Hyde, one of Hollywood's most influential agents, saw Marilyn – and fell in love. He knew he hadn't long to live, and wanted to marry Marilyn so that she would inherit his fortune. Marilyn refused; she felt it wrong to marry a man she was not in love with. She recalled, 'I didn't regret the $1 million I turned down. I never stopped regretting the loss of Johnny Hyde.'*

Left: *Before his death, Johnny Hyde secured for Marilyn her first 'real' role. The film was John Huston's crime thriller* The Asphalt Jungle *(1950). Marilyn played Angela, the beautiful girlfriend of crooked lawyer Louis Calhern. It was an excellent film that attracted much press coverage, and* Photoplay *noticed 'a beautiful blonde . . . [who] makes the most of her footage.' The public noticed her too, and wondered who she was. Furthermore, director Joseph Mankiewicz noticed her, and decided she would be perfect for the role of Miss Caswell in his* All About Eve *(1950).*

Above: *Marilyn and cameraman Milton Krasner at work on Fox's* All About Eve. *Celeste Holm, one of the film's stars, tells of Marilyn beginning as she was to go on — an hour late on set on her first day, and needing 25 retakes to get a couple of lines right. It's hard to imagine Bette Davis, the film's star, allowing that. Marilyn played Miss Caswell, a blonde bombshell who intends to get her name in theatrical lights without being encumbered by talent. Fox production chief Darryl Zanuck was impressed enough to say 'Who's that girl? Why haven't we got her under contract?' A new contract was drawn up.*

Above: *Just staying inside her dress long enough to receive the Henrietta Award for the Best Young Box Office Personality of 1951. Fox hadn't found any more good parts for her, but they let the public look at her in* The Fireball *(1950),* Right Cross *(1950),* Hometown Story *(1951),* As Young As You Feel *(1951) and* Let's Make It Legal *(1951).*

Right: *Goodness knows what poor Marilyn was being asked to pose for here. Cooking was not something she was to go down in history for, but she tried. Her first husband, Jim Dougherty, loved her in spite of her cooking; however, she did learn to make spaghetti for Joe DiMaggio, and borsch for Arthur Miller.*

Left: *This picture of Marilyn by Bacharach was taken when she was loaned to RKO studios for* Clash By Night *(1952).*

Right: *January 1952 – working with dialogue director Tony Jowitt on the script of* We're Not Married. *The story told of five couples who learn that they weren't legally married. Marilyn plays Annabel who has just won the 'Mrs Mississippi' contest. Husband Jeff, who is feeling neglected, is delighted to learn they're not married – because it means she can't enter for 'Mrs America.' However, Annabel goes one better – she wins 'Miss Mississippi.' Not a great movie; the best the critics could manage for Marilyn was to praise her appearance and say she 'performed her role well.'*

Left: *This potato sack owed its existence to the almost topless gown Marilyn wore to receive her Henrietta Award for Best Young Box Office Personality. That one hadn't gone down too well with the press. Marilyn read one columnist who '. . . wrote that I was cheap and vulgar in it, and that I would've looked better in a potato sack.' The publicity department seized gleefully on this idea. They commissioned a tailor-made sack dress and photographer Earl Theisen to shoot Marilyn in it. It was a brilliant gimmick. Hundreds of newspapers, all across the country, featured one or other of the potato-sack pictures.*

Right: *In March 1952 the 'Golden Dreams' nude-calendar story broke. After being dropped by Columbia, Marilyn was so broke she couldn't afford her rent; and then, the last straw, her car was repossessed. So when photographer-friend Tom Kelley offered her $50 to pose nude for him she agreed. Fox told her to deny everything, but Marilyn confessed. The public loved the story, and it did her no harm at all.*

Left: Life *magazine featured Marilyn for the first time on its cover on 7 April 1952. The photographer was Philippe Halsman, whose opinion of Marilyn as a model had greatly improved. He was to say 'I know few actresses who have this incredible talent for communicating with a camera lens. She would try to seduce a camera as if it were a human being.'*

Above: *Loaned out to RKO for* Clash By Night *(1952), Marilyn played Barbara Stanwyck's brother's girl friend in this taut drama. It was her first dramatic role of any size.* The New York World Telegram and Sun *review said of Marilyn: 'This girl has a refreshing exuberance . . . She is a forceful actress, too, when crisis comes along. She has definitely stamped herself as a gifted new star.'*

Above: *While at Columbia, Marilyn had so impressed Natasha Lytess, the studio's drama coach, that, shortly afterward, Lytess left her job to become Marilyn's private coach. Marilyn also lived with her for some time. In due course she arranged for Lytess to be employed by Fox. Most of Marilyn's directors dreaded the sight of Lytess at the edge of their sets; it was her thumbs down – not theirs – that made Marilyn demand yet another retake. Then in 1956, after meeting Paula Strasberg of the 'Method' Actors Studio, Marilyn dropped Lytess very abruptly – by telegram.*

Above: Don't Bother To Knock (1952) was a very strange
choice for Fox to have made for Marilyn's first starring role,
for she played a psychotic baby-sitter who first endangers
her charge and then threatens suicide – an unusual role for a
blonde bombshell. Her reviews were very mixed, and the film
was not a hit. However, the public certainly wasn't ready to
write her off. Co-star Anne Bancroft found acting with
Marilyn 'remarkable,' and said of her 'suicide' scene: 'It was
so real. I responded. I really reacted to her. She moved me
so that the tears came into my eyes.'

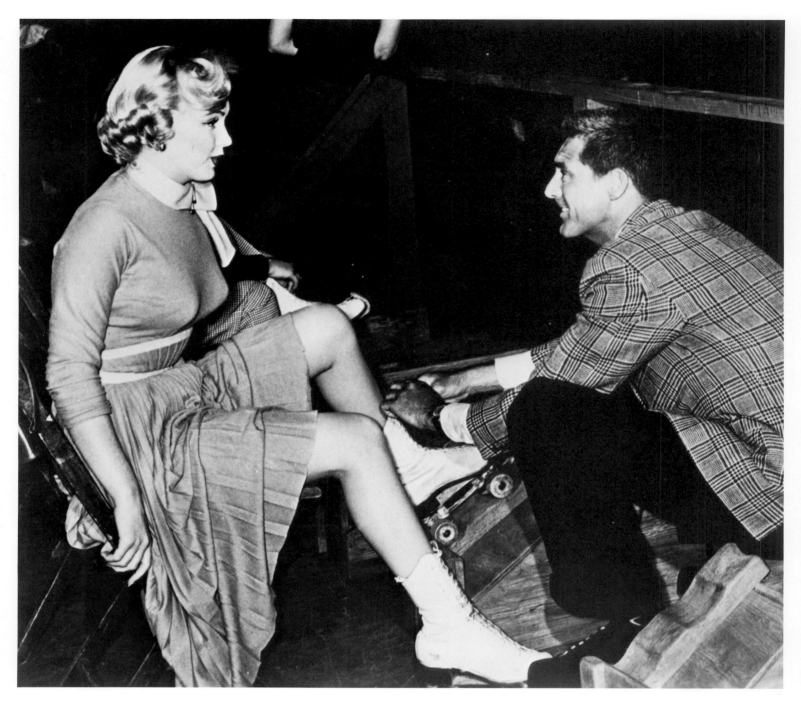

Above: In Monkey Business (1952), Cary Grant played a scientist who accidentally drinks his own youth potion – and runs off to rollerskate with his boss's secretary (Marilyn). It was a role that only gave the critics her physical attributes to comment on, which they all did. So did America's baseball hero, Joe DiMaggio, who finally managed to meet her – on a blind date. Marilyn had envisaged someone slick, loud and flashy – but she liked the man she met. It was the beginning of a news-headlining romance.

Right: Niagara (1953) showcased Marilyn as a scheming blonde out to dispose of her gloomy, jealous husband (Joseph Cotton). Marilyn is so 'hot' in this film that when she sits crooning to her favorite record 'Kiss,' the ground beneath her sizzles. Cotton commented, 'Everything that girl does is so sexy.' Marilyn was superb as a femme fatale; sad that this side of her talent wasn't developed. This is the film also famous for Marilyn's 'horizontal' walk – filmed lovingly by director Henry Hathaway from the rear.

Above: *While waiting for her next movie role, Marilyn was kept busy by the studio, the press and the public, and posed for many of these pool-side shots. Then in September 1952 she was asked to be Grand Marshal at the 'Miss America' pageant. Unfortunately, it was another occasion on which Marilyn's decolletage earned her more criticism than admiration. However, she redeemed herself a few months later by winning the* Redbook *Award for Best Young Box Office Personality.*

Right: *Marilyn was finally playing a role that could have been written for her: Lorelei Lee, the heroine of Anita Loos's* Gentlemen Prefer Blondes. *Though Loos had written her book in the 1920s, the character of this seemingly witless but in fact exceedingly shrewd 'baby-faced blonde whose eyes open for diamonds and close for kisses' updated beautifully to the Fifties. Marilyn's co-star was RKO's glamorous Jane Russell. The two women worked well together, despite the press's efforts to fabricate a feud between them.*

Left: *Time out from shooting to pick up another award – the* Photoplay Award for Fastest Rising Star of 1952 *– and another round of abuse for appearing 'cheap and vulgar.' This time it was led by Joan Crawford – an actress Marilyn highly esteemed – and apparently seconded by Joe DiMaggio. He seems to have believed that his interest in Marilyn meant that the rest of the world should stop looking at her. The dress in dispute was, in fact, a gold lamé gown from* Gentlemen Prefer Blondes, *into which Marilyn had been sewn by Billy Travilla, the studio's costume designer.*

Right: *Marilyn responded to Joan Crawford's attack on her for affronting a public who 'likes to know that underneath it all . . . actresses are ladies' in the gossip column of Hollywood's 'First Lady of the Press' – Louella Parsons. Marilyn spoke – either with inside knowledge or prophetic irony – of how she had always admired Crawford for being a wonderful mother. Parsons championed Marilyn from the outset, and was one of the most powerful friends any Hollywood actress could hope to have.*

Above: *Howard Hawks had much to endure on* Gentlemen Prefer Blondes *(1953). There was Marilyn's ever-escalating lateness – no joke on a musical when a large cast of dancers, singers and musicians was having to kill time. He also had a showdown with Marilyn's drama coach Natasha Lytess over the number of retakes she demanded. But the film's release proved once and for all that Marilyn was the blonde gentlemen preferred.*

Left: *Marilyn was an all-round success in Gentlemen Prefer Blondes. Her version of 'Diamonds Are A Girl's Best Friend' has become an acknowledged classic, and her work with Jane Russell on the other show-stopping musical numbers was teaming at its best. The picture was a huge box-office hit, and is still many people's favorite Marilyn movie.*

Above: How To Marry A Millionaire *(1953) was shot in the new CinemaScope process – an odd choice for widescreen, as so much of the film takes place in an apartment. This is the movie in which Marilyn proved she looked just as gorgeous in glasses. Her co-stars were Lauren Bacall (right) and Betty Grable (center). Bacall found working with Marilyn hard: 'A scene often went to 15 or more takes . . . not easy . . . She was always late, but I think it was in terror. She couldn't face what she was being called upon to do.'*

Above: *On 26 June 1953 Marilyn and Jane Russell were invited to press their hands and feet in wet cement – thus adding their prints to the famous collection in the forecourt of Grauman's Chinese Theater. Marilyn felt a bust-print and a buttock-print would be better, but no one had the courage to take her up on it.*

Left: *Marilyn made her television debut in 'The Jack Benny Show.' In this episode, Benny had a wonderful dream in which Marilyn confesses that, now she has met him, she wants him more than money or even diamonds.*

Left: *The next stop for Marilyn was Canada – to film a Western,* River Of No Return *(1954), with director Otto Preminger and co-star Robert Mitchum, who she had first met when he worked alongside her then husband Jim Dougherty at the Lockheed Aircraft factory.*

Above: *Marilyn's role in* The River Of No Return *was that of a saloon-singer who, after a series of largely cold and wet adventures, is romantically carried off by Mitchum to live with him and his son on his farm. This allowed her to delight her public in both saloon-girl glamour and tight blue jeans. Marilyn's opinion of the film – 'a Z cowboy movie in which acting finished third to the scenery and CinemaScope' – is hard to fault.*

Above: *Marilyn was soon to be joined on location for* River Of No Return *by Joe DiMaggio. He would do some fishing while she was shooting. The couple still hadn't set a wedding date. Meanwhile, tension reigned in Alberta, as director Preminger chided Marilyn for her lateness and vagueness — and banished drama coach Lytess from the set. Marilyn retaliated by claiming to have broken a leg, and escaped behind crutches.*

Left: *Marilyn cutting the 'birthday' cake at a party to celebrate the first anniversary of CinemaScope. Indeed, she was the original CinemaScope star.* How To Marry A Millionaire *(1953) was the first film to be shot in CinemaScope (even though* The Robe *was the first to be released), and her next four films all featured the new widescreen process.*

Above: *Joe DiMaggio and his long-time friend Frank Sinatra together caused the scandal known as the 'Wrong Door Raid.' After DiMaggio and Marilyn broke up, Joe remained jealous of her friends, and he and Sinatra planned a raid to 'catch her in the act.' However, the raid went to the wrong door. Sinatra and DiMaggio had to compensate the wrong door's outraged owner. After the DiMaggio divorce, Marilyn and Sinatra dated for a while, which hurt Joe. Sinatra was Marilyn's favorite singer. She was listening to his records on the night she died.*

Above: *Married at last, on 14 January 1954, Marilyn and Joe chose to honeymoon in Japan – where Joe had many baseball fans. But the US Army was waiting there for its favorite pinup, to see if she would entertain the American troops in Korea. Marilyn enchanted tens of thousands as she performed 'Diamonds Are A Girl's Best Friend,' 'Bye Bye Baby,' 'Somebody Love Me' and 'Kiss Me Again' – a variation on 'Do It Again,' because someone in command thought the lyrics dangerously suggestive.*

Right: *Marilyn worked for four days in Korea, traveling by jeep and helicopter, doing 10 shows and entertaining over 100,000 men. She said as she left: 'This was the best thing that ever happened to me.' Most of the time she was wearing the skimpiest of dresses in bitingly cold winds and returned to Japan with mild pneumonia which Joe had to nurse for four days before they could resume their holiday.*

Left: *One of Sam Shaw's famous shots of Marilyn. Mrs DiMaggio had, as it happened, plenty of time for leisurely baths because she had been suspended by Fox for refusing to make* The Girl In Pink Tights. *Marilyn was beginning to rebel against the studio. She later said, 'They never ask my opinion. They just tell me what time to come to work.'*

Below: *Alan Ladd presents Marilyn with* Photoplay *magazine's Best Actress gold medal for her performances in* Gentlemen Prefer Blondes *and* How To Marry A Millionaire. *Although she received many awards for her acting – as well as scores of personality awards – Marilyn was never even nominated for an Oscar.*

Left: *When the hottest 'item' in Hollywood finally got married on 14 January 1954 in San Francisco (Joe's home town), Marilyn, for her wedding dress, could not have conceded further to DiMaggio's disapproval of her usual line in revealing gowns. They clearly loved one another: he was her protector, she was his baby-doll. But the following nine months would show that they were one of those couples who just couldn't live together. Furthermore, Joe did have much to be jealous of, for Marilyn doesn't seem to have seen faithfulness as something that anyone should expect of her.*

These pages: *Why did Marilyn ever agree to make* There's No Business Like Show Business *(1954)? It seems she was promised* The Seven Year Itch *if she did. It was a show-business story, co-starring Donald O'Connor (left), Mitzi Gaynor (right), Ethel Merman, Dan Dailey and Johnnie Ray as The Five Donahues. Donald falls for an aspiring revue artiste, Marilyn, and arranges for her to perform 'Heat Wave' on their next program. Given the tackiness of Marilyn's costume and choreographed gyrations, it's not surprising that mother Merman was not impressed.*

Left: *The famous skirt-blowing scene from* The Seven Year Itch *(1955). This was director Billy Wilder's first comedy with Marilyn, in which she played 'The Girl Upstairs' who is a sore temptation to Tom Ewell – alone in the flat below while his wife and son are away for the summer. Shooting took place in New York, and, although the skirt scene was shot at 1.00 am, hundreds of spectators turned up to watch. Marilyn was wearing a very respectable pair of white panties for the occasion. As she observed, 'Gee, imagine if they had let me dress the way I really do! Wouldn't that have been something . . .? But what good is being a sex star if it drives your man away?'*

Above: *Joe DiMaggio was deeply upset by* The Seven Year Itch *skirt-blowing scene. He stood, white-faced, watching take after take, as Marilyn's skirt swirled over her head. Within a month the couple were officially separated and a few weeks later, on 27 October 1954, the divorce was granted. However, they remained good friends; indeed, Joe may have been her best friend. Here, on 1 June 1955, her birthday, he escorts her to the film's premiere – a courageous act given that huge cardboard cut-outs of the skirt scene were everywhere.*

Below: 'Whitey' Snyder working on Marilyn's makeup before the shooting of a scene in River Of No Return. Snyder reported that Marilyn herself had 'makeup tricks that nobody else has . . . and no other actress can do.'

The New Marilyn

ven though *The Seven Year Itch* was a huge criti-
cal and commercial success, Fox still refused to
see Marilyn as someone whose feelings and
opinions were worth listening to. So Marilyn mutinied
against the next dumb-blonde part they assigned her,
and by Chistmas she had moved East. On 7 January
1955, Marilyn, looking absolutely radiant, announced to
a press conference that she and her new partner Milton
Greene had formed Marilyn Monroe Productions – 'So I
can play the better kind of roles I want to play.' Marilyn
moved into New York's Waldorf Astoria hotel. She and
DiMaggio spent much of the rest of the year trying to
patch up their marriage – but the divorce was eventually decreed in November.

In August Marilyn began work at the Actors Studio
which was headed by Lee and Paula Strasberg of
Method Acting fame. The Strasbergs described her as
one of the greatest raw acting talents they had ever en-
countered. It was extremely courageous for such a big
movie star to expose herself to the judgment of
'serious' actors, but it was worth it. John Huston
observed, on *The Misfits*, 'I found that, despite her
problems . . . she had become an actress who acted
from the inside out, someone who had to feel it in her in-
sides before she could perform.'

The other main call on her time in the East was playwright Arthur Miller. Opinion is sharply divided as to
whether Miller's marriage was already on the wane or
whether it dissolved in the face of Marilyn's single-
minded determination to become Mrs Miller.

Then, in February 1956, Marilyn Monroe Productions
announced their first picture – *The Prince And The
Showgirl*, co-starring and directed by Laurence Olivier,
and to be filmed in England. Olivier referred to Marilyn
as 'a brilliant comedienne, which to me means she is
also an extremely skilled actress.'

Thereafter she returned to Hollywood, having agreed
a new contract with Fox. In addition to her own company's films she undertook to make four Fox films
during the next seven years, and they undertook to pay
her $100,000 per picture, plus a back-payment of
$100,000. She had approval of story, director, camera-
man and makeup man, and Fox also agreed to pay
$500 a week toward the costs of an analyst, a secre-
tary, a maid, an acting coach – and an analyst. Marilyn
was by this time seeing an analyst regularly. In spite of
her superstardom, she was often depressed, uncertain
and lonely. And she had, of course, a family history of
mental illness to contend with.

Her first new contract film was *Bus Stop*, directed by
Joshua Logan. Marilyn played saloon-singer Cherie,
with whom an enthusiatic young rancher falls in love
when he arrives in town for a rodeo. Joshua Logan,
who had doubts about Marilyn's ability before shooting
began, was saying by the end, 'I found her to be one of
the greatest talents of all time . . . the most constantly
exciting actress I ever worked with.' Marilyn got her
warmest reviews thus far for *Bus Stop*. Critics who had
previously only praised her figure now acknowledged
her as a fine actress.

On 1 July 1956, Miller and Marilyn were married – 'the
Hourglass to the Egghead.' She was clearly head-over-
heels in love. Two weeks later they were off to London
for *The Prince And The Showgirl*.

Work on that film was far from easy. Laurence Olivier
didn't have the knack of handling Marilyn; he didn't
understand her problems and couldn't see why the
crew should endure hours of waiting for her to appear,
or endless retakes that he, as director, thought un-
necessary. But, everyone agreed that her rushes were
wonderful. Dame Sybil Thorndike, one of her co-stars,
told Olivier that Marilyn knew more about film acting
than any of them. Many American critics didn't like *The
Prince And The Showgirl*, but the Italians and the
French gave her their equivalents of a Best Foreign
Actress Oscar.

Throughout this time Marilyn was actively supporting
Miller who was being tried by the House Un-American
Activities Committee for communist sympathies. However, she didn't feel that Miller had supported her in her
battles with Olivier.

In the spring of 1957 she bought out her share of
Marilyn Monroe Productions from Milton Greene with
whom her relations had become increasingly strained.
By now Marilyn was trying hard to have a baby (many
previous abortions would contribute to making this difficult), but this attempt resulted in an ectopic pregnancy
after which she needed months of rest.

April 1958 found her back at work again, on Billy
Wilder's *Some Like It Hot* with Tony Curtis and Jack
Lemmon. Wilder found her much harder work on this
film. Whole days would be wasted trying to get her to
come out of her dressing room. Marilyn's being pregnant again certainly didn't help – and, sadly, she was to
lose this baby too. Yet, on 8 March 1960, Marilyn was
awarded the Golden Globe Award as Best Actress in a
Comedy for her performance as Sugar Kane, the singer
in *Some Like It Hot*.

Left: *Sam Shaw's picture of Marilyn looking very much at home in New York was in fact taken while there on location for* The Seven Year Itch. *But Marilyn would soon make New York her home. The fact that her last film had been an enormous success inspired Fox to offer her nothing finer than a nonentity called* How To Be Very, Very Popular. *Marilyn refused to do it. In January 1955 Marilyn held a press conference to announce the formation of her own company, Marilyn Monroe Productions Inc – 'so I can play the better kinds of roles I want to play.' Her partner was photographer Milton Greene whom she had met some 18 months earlier. Fox responded to Marilyn's announcement by suspending her, but by then Marilyn had already suspended herself and moved to New York. Greene resigned his $50,000-a-year job on* Look *magazine to take charge of her affairs. He also negotiated a new, and greatly improved, contract for Marilyn with Fox, and went back to Hollywood with her in 1956.*

Above: Marion Brando accompanies Marilyn to the premiere of The Rose Tattoo *in 1955. Marilyn described him as 'one of the most attractive men I ever met.' It seems likely that Brando and Marilyn had an affair, one that ceased when her liaison with Arthur Miller became public knowledge. They were further linked by Lee Strasberg, head of the Actors Studio, who described them as the two greatest raw talents he had ever worked with.*

Right: Marilyn was determined to become a serious actress, so she headed for the Actors Studio – home of The Method. Marilyn was only enlisted as an observer at the school; it took several auditions over a period of time to become a member, and Marilyn didn't stay long enough for that. However, her performance there of an excerpt from Anna Christie, *with Maureen Stapleton, deeply impressed all who saw it. Many were skeptical of her acting ambitions, but directors whom she later worked with could see how much Marilyn had learned.*

Above: *In February 1956 Marilyn returned to Hollywood. However, her first major appearance there was at a press conference with Milton Greene, vice-president of Marilyn Monroe Productions, and studio boss Jack L Warner to announce their forthcoming co-production.* The Prince And The Showgirl *would star Marilyn Monroe and Laurence Olivier, who would also co-produce and direct, and would be filmed in England.*

Right: *Marilyn's first new-contract film for Fox was* Bus Stop *(1956), directed by Joshua Logan. She played Cherie, a third-rate saloon-singer, and her almost tuneless version of 'That Old Black Magic' – in an appalling fish-net costume, and with dreadful gestures and lighting – is superb. Her unglowing, pasty complexion was designed for her by Milton Greene. Marilyn now had Paula Strasberg from the Actors Studio as her drama coach instead of Natasha Lytess.*

Left: *For Cherie in* Bus Stop *Marilyn produced a comic performance of flair, charm and pathos. The critics were stunned and said: 'The girl is a terrific comedienne . . . a revelation,' and 'Marilyn Monroe has finally proved herself an actress,' and 'she gives a performance . . . that marks her as a genuine acting star.' However, once again no one thought of nominating her for an Oscar.*

Right: *Marilyn had first met playwright Arthur Miller – a married man with two children – in 1950. When she moved to New York he sought her out and they dated 'in secret' until the press noticed. In June 1956 Miller obtained a divorce and announced that he and Marilyn would be married before leaving for England in July to start* The Prince And The Showgirl. *Marilyn clearly adored him. She said 'This is the first time I think I've been really in love,' and 'We're so congenial!'*

Left: *'The Egghead and the Hourglass' were wed – in two ceremonies: a civil one on 29 June and a Jewish one (Marilyn had converted to Judaism) on 1 July 1956. For Marilyn, it meant the world now had to take her seriously: 'If I were nothing but a dumb blonde, he wouldn't have married me.'*

Left: *Marilyn on her way to a Royal Command Film Performance some three months after arriving in England – complete with new husband (Arthur Miller), company vice-president and wife (Milton and Amy Greene), drama coach and husband (Paula and Lee Strasberg), and some 27 pieces of baggage.*

Right: *Marilyn is presented to Queen Elizabeth II in the Empire Theatre, London, while at a Royal Command Film Performance of* The Battle Of The River Plate. *Her Majesty had commented approvingly on Marilyn's 'very proper curtsey.' Marilyn replied that she'd learned how to curtsey for her new film, and no longer found it difficult.*

Left: *Laurence Olivier and Marilyn had first met when he joined her at a New York press conference in February 1956 to announce their forthcoming film together. It was to be based on Terence Rattigan's play* The Sleeping Prince – *a title that was later changed for the film's American release to* The Prince And The Showgirl. *In the middle of the conference, something came adrift. 'How did it feel when the strap broke?' asked a reporter, which was a snide reference to Marilyn's recent Method Acting training. She was not amused.*

Left: *The work stresses of The Prince And The Showgirl also put the Miller marriage under severe strain. Miller had to become a full-time nursemaid. Marilyn began to see his efforts to get her to the set as his working for 'them' – Olivier and the film's production staff. In addition, Marilyn was deeply upset about an entry she found in Miller's notebook: 'It was something about how disappointed he was in me. How he thought I was some kind of angel, but now he guessed he was wrong.' Marilyn felt hurt and betrayed, for Miller's sympathies no longer seemed to lie with her, but with Olivier.*

Left: *Olivier had already glimpsed the Marilyn he was going to have to deal with, for she was an hour late for her press conference in New York, and an hour late for his London one. He did not find the key to working with Marilyn. The trouble probably was that he treated her like a professional actress – instead of a film star. On the first day of shooting Olivier said, 'All right, Marilyn. Be sexy.' She ran off the set, distraught, and thereafter resorted to champagne and sleeping pills to overcome her inability to communicate with him. There were many days when Miller was unable to rouse her enough to get her to the studio.*

Right: The Prince And The Showgirl *was finally finished; indeed, Milton Greene somehow managed to bring it in under budget. Marilyn asked the cast and crew to forgive her behavior: 'I've been very, very sick all through the picture. Please, please don't hold it against me.' Some of the critics loved her as Elsie – the kittenish showgirl who wins the heart of the Prince Regent of Carpathia (Olivier); some had reservations. Nevertheless, Marilyn earned for her performance the David di Donatello Prize (Italy's Oscar) and the Crystal Star Award (France's Oscar) for Best Foreign Actress.*

Above: *A picture – one of a series taken by Cecil Beaton in 1956 – that was one of Marilyn's personal favorites.*

Right: *While in England Marilyn and Miller attended the opening of his new play A View From The Bridge. Marilyn later said of Miller: 'He is a wonderful writer, a brilliant man. But I think he is a better writer than a husband.'*

Left: *Although he had
become Marilyn's business
partner, Milton Greene
remained a superb
photographer – as can be
seen in this picture from his
'black hat and fish-nets'
series of 1956.*

Below: *It seems that
however famous, wealthy
or influential a movie star
Marilyn became, she would
never be completely safe
from this kind of leopard-
skin-rug publicity.*

Below: *Marilyn again by her photographer-partner Milton Greene. In the spring of 1957 Marilyn bought Greene out. Relations between them had become very strained; some feel this was because Miller distrusted and disliked him. However, Greene had backed Marilyn during her long 'holiday' in New York. He also negotiated her new Fox contract which gave her, at last, a decent salary and approval of stories and directors.*

Right: 'Whitey' Snyder was a part of 'the Marilyn story' from beginning to end. It was he who did her makeup for her first screen test – and it was he who, at Marilyn's special, long-arranged request, did her makeup for her funeral. In between, he was for many years one of her best and most trusted friends and closest confidants. Whitey remembers, 'The trouble with Marilyn was she didn't trust her own judgment, always had someone around to depend on. Coaches, so-called friends. Even me.'

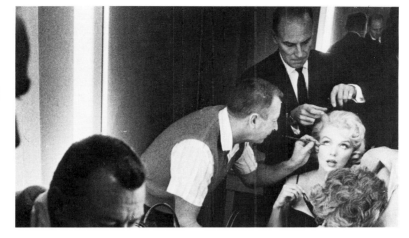

Below: Marilyn in the Millers' country home. During less fraught moments Miller was working on the story that would become his script for Marilyn – The Misfits.

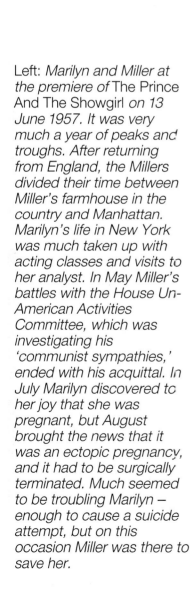

Left: Marilyn and Miller at the premiere of The Prince And The Showgirl on 13 June 1957. It was very much a year of peaks and troughs. After returning from England, the Millers divided their time between Miller's farmhouse in the country and Manhattan. Marilyn's life in New York was much taken up with acting classes and visits to her analyst. In May Miller's battles with the House Un-American Activities Committee, which was investigating his 'communist sympathies,' ended with his acquittal. In July Marilyn discovered to her joy that she was pregnant, but August brought the news that it was an ectopic pregnancy, and it had to be surgically terminated. Much seemed to be troubling Marilyn – enough to cause a suicide attempt, but on this occasion Miller was there to save her.

Left: *One of a series of pictures photographer Philippe Halsman took of Marilyn in 1959.*

Right: *On 4 August 1958 Marilyn began work on* Some Like It Hot *(1959). This was director Billy Wilder's story of two musicians – Tony Curtis and Jack Lemmon (right) – who are innocent witnesses to the St Valentine's Day Massacre and have to escape by disguising themselves as members of a girls' jazz band. Marilyn played the band's singer – Sugar Kane. Wilder persuaded her to let him shoot the film in black-and-white (her contract stipulated only color), otherwise the boys' powder and lipstick was going to look grotesque.*

Left: *Marilyn with drama coaches Lee and Paula Strasberg. Marilyn asked Lee about* Some Like It Hot. *How could she act with two men in drag as if they were really close girl friends? Lee reminded her that women friends were hard for her to make because they were often jealous: 'Now, here, suddenly, are two women and they want to be your friend . . . And I remember from there on . . . the movie worked for her.' Lemmon, who made a delightful girl, did become a good friend. He was very tolerant of her lateness and her retakes.*

Left: *Photographer Philippe Halsman catching Marilyn in a sparkling, carefree moment.*

Right: *Filming* Some Like It Hot *was fraught with production problems. Billy Wilder was exasperated with Marilyn's unprofessionalism. It sometimes took days to get her out of her dressing room. Marilyn got pregnant again, and Miller accused Wilder's production schedules of causing her to have another miscarriage. Yet, she is absolutely luminous in the finished film. The critics said 'She's a comedienne with that combination of sex appeal and timing that just can't be beat,' and 'Marilyn does herself proud, giving a performance of such intrinsic quality that you begin to believe she's only being herself.'*

Left: *Marilyn at the start-of-filming party for* Some Like It Hot *with Tony Curtis (left) and George Raft (right). The film provoked a famous exchange between Curtis and Marilyn. He was infuriated by all her retakes; by the time she'd got it right, he had long since passed his peak. On being asked how it felt to be able to spend so much time kissing Marilyn, he replied 'Kissing her is like kissing Hitler' – a grim testament from a Jew. Marilyn replied benignly, 'He's just jealous because I got to wear prettier dresses than he did.'*

Right: *Marilyn at work on* Let's Make Love *– a film distinguished by little other than Marilyn's rendition of 'My Heart Belongs To Daddy.'*

Something Had to Give

When Marilyn began work with Yves Montand on *Let's Make Love*, trouble in the Miller marriage was already brewing. Marilyn and Montand started an affair, but, as soon as it became too public, Montand (married to the very tolerant Simone Signoret) backed off. Marilyn, who had been deeply smitten, was shocked by his easy rejection of her.

Meantime, Miller had written a script for Marilyn – *The Misfits* (1960). It drew extensively on the Marilyn Miller felt he knew. She was happy at the prospect of working with Clark Gable – an actor she had always admired and the man she used to dream of having been her real father. Miller wrote for Marilyn the role of Roslyn – newly divorced, vulnerable, lonely, appalled by cruelty to animals – who, with her companion (Thelma Ritter), falls in with a group of cowboys: Gable, Montgomery Clift and Eli Wallach.

Tensions on the set were running high. Miller and Marilyn were drifting further apart. Director John Huston and Miller reshaped Marilyn's role almost daily. Marilyn got more anxious, more difficult and more dependent on pills and alcohol. Eventually she was taken off to hospital to recover from 'acute exhaustion.' Huston had to devise endless ways of shooting round her in the ferocious heat of the Nevada desert. It was all too much for Gable who died of a heart attack in November 1960, only days after shooting ended.

Although it was not a box-office success, the critics thought that the *The Misfits* was excellent, that Gable had never been better, and that Marilyn was superb. Later that November Marilyn announced to the press that her marriage to Miller was over. By the following March she was so emotionally distressed that her psychiatrist placed her in the Payne Whitney Psychiatric Clinic in New York. There she found herself behind locked doors and barred windows. She finally persuaded the authorities to let her phone Joe DiMaggio, who took her away to the Columbia Presbyterian Medical Center. 'Thank God for Joe!' said Marilyn, and began to see him more and more often.

The first months of 1962 brought news of Arthur Miller's remarriage. More positive for Marilyn was the purchase of her very first home. It was a modest little Spanish-style house, but it did have its own swimming pool – of which she was very proud.

Professionally, life was looking extremely promising. In March she received a Golden Globe Award for being the world's most popular star. In April she began work on another movie – *Something's Got To Give* with Dean Martin as her co-star and George Cukor as her director. Marilyn had approved the initial script, but Cukor began commissioning drastic revisions. Marilyn retaliated by repeatedly failing to turn up for work. At one point she flew to New York to sing 'Happy Birthday Mr President' at John Kennedy's birthday party. Marilyn returned to the highly dispirited set of *Something's Got To Give*. Then she was 'off sick' again – and the studio decided to call a halt to its now enormous losses. Marilyn was fired.

Marilyn's 'intimate relationships' with both John and Bobby Kennedy were rumors that now seem to be confirmed beyond all doubt. Actor Peter Lawford, then married to their sister Pat Kennedy had a beach home in Santa Monica where these two Kennedy brothers could conduct their West Coast liaisons in secrecy. When John was based in the East, it seems that he met Marilyn in New York at the Carlyle Hotel.

John Kennedy appears to have already cooled off his friendship with Marilyn; but throughout the month of July Marilyn persisted in trying to contact Bobby at the Justice Department. He, too, seems to have been pulling away. It also seems quite probable that she had yet another abortion in those last months.

On 5 August 1962, a shocked world learned that Marilyn Monroe had died. Joe DiMaggio organized the funeral and, in his bitterness, debarred most of Marilyn's Hollywood friends from the service. He didn't consider them true friends.

Years of investigation by many people have failed to determine whether it was an accidental overdose, a suicide or murder. The discrepancies in the evidence, the factors that were never examined in the autopsy, and the extraordinarily unorthodox way that events after her death were handled certainly point to a massive cover-up, but it may simply have been the Kennedy connection that was being misted over. On the other hand, she may have been an innocent pawn in a grim plot to wreck the Kennedys – or she may just have been getting too talkative. The truth will probably never be known; though the official findings were that Marilyn took an overdose of drugs.

What is known is that Marilyn was, when a camera was turned upon her, a magical lady. She had a hundred smiles, each more heart-stopping than the last. She was a fountain of fun; she was also a pool of deep sorrow. She has left, on film, huge helpings of joy. She has left, on the human soul, an indelible mark. She is a true Hollywood myth.

Above: Let's Make Love *didn't have much to offer Marilyn.
The story was rather dreary, and she didn't look her usual
dazzling self. Her costumes were unflattering, and didn't
conceal the fact that she was, for Marilyn, a trifle pudgy. She
had several numbers to sing, including 'Let's Make Love,'
'Incurably Romantic' and 'Specialization.' However, the
number that stands out is her show-stopping version of Cole
Porter's 'My Heart Belongs To Daddy.'*

Right: *Yves Montand had started his career as the 'protégé' of Edith Piaf, and subsequently married French actress Simone Signoret. Both Signoret and Miller had business out of town during the filming of Let's Make Love, whereupon Marilyn and Montand quickly became a 'romantic item' in the press. The Millers' relationship was, in any case, already floundering; but Montand had no intention of endangering his marriage. As Marilyn got warmer, he retreated, saying: 'Perhaps I was too tender . . . Perhaps she had a schoolgirl crush. If she did, I'm sorry.' It was at this moment that Signoret was awarded an Oscar for Room At The Top.*

Below: *Let's Make Love was a big disappointment – both as a film and as a step forward in Marilyn's career. Marilyn and Montand's relationship proved even less successful onscreen than it had been off.*

Left: *Marilyn at work on* Let's Make Love *(1960) with British song-and-dance man Frankie Vaughan. Her co-star was French heartthrob Yves Montand. Marilyn had been unhappy with much of the script, and got Miller to rework it for her. As a result, Gregory Peck, Cary Grant, Charlton Heston and Rock Hudson all turned down the lead. At that point Marilyn went to see Montand's one-man show on Broadway – and signed him up.*

Above: *Gene Kelly (center) had a guest spot in the film, which told the story of a billionaire (Yves Montand) who, on learning that he is to be lampooned in an off-Broadway review, goes to a rehearsal – and is hired (unrecognized) to play himself. He then meets and falls in love with Marilyn, one of the cast. He hires Kelly to teach him how to dance, Bing Crosby to teach him to sing, and Milton Berle to show him how to be funny.*

Left: *On 18 July 1960 filming began on* The Misfits. *Marilyn's leading men were Clark Gable (right), Montgomery Clift (front left), and Eli Wallach (behind Clift). Miller (back) wrote the screenplay, and the director was John Huston (behind Marilyn). Marilyn plays Roslyn, a newly divorced girl who brings a breath of hope to a bunch of cowboys and drifters.*

Right: *It was over 110°F in the Nevada desert, the location for* The Misfits. *Marilyn and Miller were barely communicating and the shoot was accordingly split into two camps. Playing Roslyn – so much of which was herself – devastated Marilyn and resulted in a week's hospitalization for 'exhaustion.' Although Marilyn's performance is brilliant – poignant, innocent, childlike, vulnerable – it also seems haunted, as though a ghost was already on the screen.*

Right: *Marilyn talking to Huston at the start-of-filming party. She was delighted to be working with Gable, whom she'd admired all her life. She called him 'a gentleman . . . The best.' Gable admired Marilyn too, thought her 'completely feminine,' but by the end of filming he was saying, 'Christ, I'm glad this picture's finished. She damn near gave me a heart attack.' And indeed Gable did die of a heart attack, only days later.*

Above: *Not one of Marilyn's happiest expressions – but a happy moment, for the Hollywood Foreign Press Association had just selected her as the winner of their Golden Globe Award for Best Actress in a Motion Picture Comedy. This was awarded for her role as Sugar Kane in* Some Like It Hot.

Gatefold: *A portrait of Marilyn taken to publicize the opening of* The Prince And The Showgirl *with Laurence Olivier.*

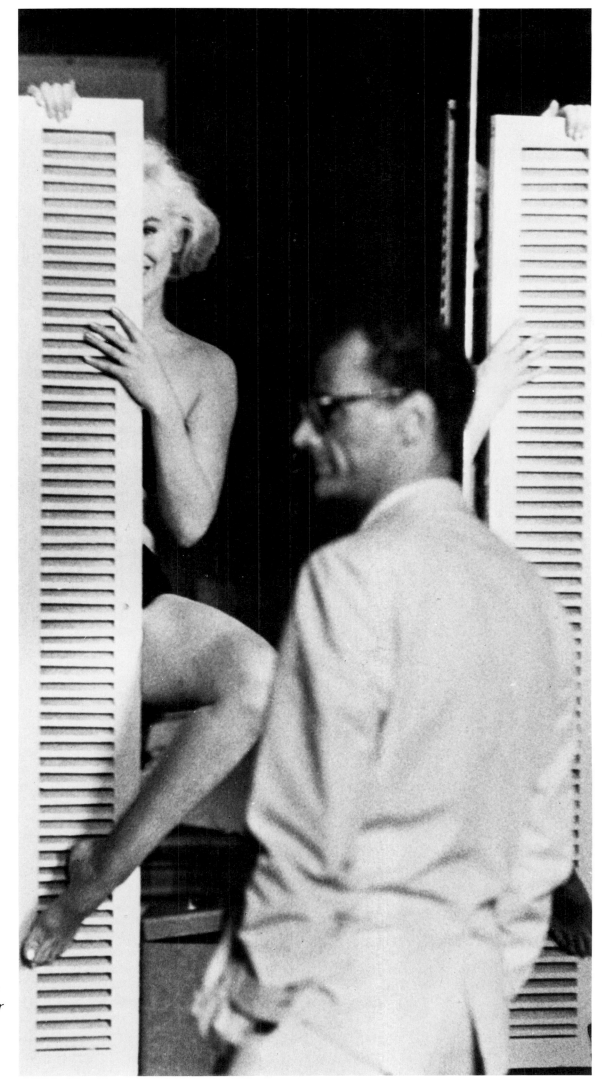

Right: *Happier days for the Millers before, on 11 November 1960, Marilyn announced to the press that her marriage to Miller was over. Their divorce came through the following January. Within a year Miller was married again, to a photographer who had been working on* The Misfits.

Above: *Marilyn's director on Let's Make Love was George Cukor, and in April 1962 they began work again, this time on Something's Got To Give, a comedy co-starring her with Dean Martin.*

Right: *On this occasion Marilyn's absence (one of many) from the set of Something's Got To Give was understandable, for she had been asked to sing 'Happy Birthday Mr President' at John Kennedy's birthday rally.*

Left: *Following her separation from Miller and the death of Clark Gable, Marilyn grew more and more depressed and increasingly dependent on pills and 'champagne.' Finally her analyst had her admitted to the Payne Whitney Psychiatric Clinic at New York Hospital for observation.*

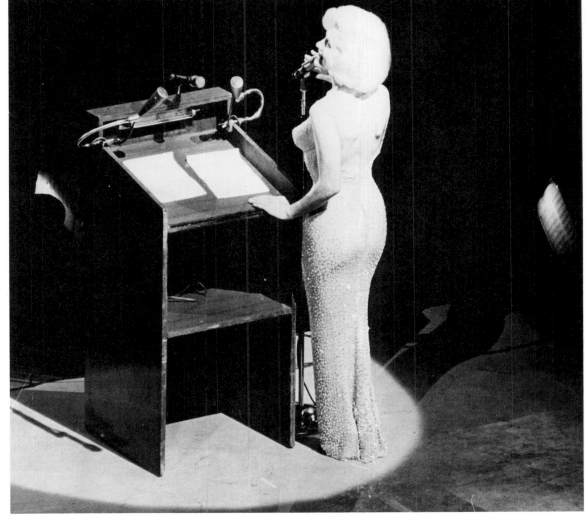

Above: 'The greatest lover in the whole wide world' was how
Marilyn described José Bolanos in 1962. She met him in
Mexico City when she was buying 'authentic' furniture for
the little Spanish hacienda that was the very first home she
had ever owned. Bolanos was himself in films in Mexico.
Here they are pictured together at the 1962 Golden Globe
Award Ceremony.

Above: *The world had not, after all, fallen out of love with Marilyn, for in March 1962, at the Hollywood Foreign Press Association's nineteenth annual dinner, she was awarded a Golden Globe Award for being the World's Favorite Actress. Rock Hudson makes the presentation.*

Left: *Shooting the famous nude swimming scene in Something's Got To Give. It was Marilyn who made it nude, by kicking off her flesh-colored swimming suit. She was always happiest when not wearing anything, and people living or working with her got very used to Marilyn wandering around with no clothes on.*

Above: *Hardly any footage of Marilyn in* Something's Got To
Give *exists, for she only turned up for work a handful of
times in six weeks of shooting. Finally, on 8 June, Fox lost its
temper, and fired her, announcing that her repeated
absences had already lost the company over half a million
dollars. The rushes that do remain show Marilyn looking
radiantly lovely.*

Left: *On 5 August 1962, Marilyn Monroe was found dead at her home on Fifth Helena Drive, Brentwood, California. An autopsy was performed that morning, and a 'psychiatric autopsy' was conducted a week or so later. Their findings were that the death was caused by drugs and that the mode of death was 'probably suicide.'*

Above: *Joe DiMaggio with Joe Jr, the son of his first marriage, beside him at the funeral of Marilyn Monroe. The funeral arrangements had been made by DiMaggio, Marilyn's half-sister Bernice Miracle and her business manager Inez Melson. The service took place on 8 August 1962 at Westwood Memorial Park Chapel.*

Below: *Marilyn had called many people on that last day. Some thought she sounded depressed; others found her quite cheerful. Was her death suicide? Was it an accidental overdose? Or had her Kennedy connections woven for her some tragic destiny?*

'What do I wear in bed?
Why, Chanel No. 5, of
course.'

'No one ever told me I was
pretty when I was a little
girl. All little girls should be
told they're pretty, even if
they aren't.'

'A career is wonderful, but
you can't curl up with it on
a cold night.'

'I'm trying to prove to
myself that I'm a person.
Then maybe I'll convince
myself that I'm an actress.'

'I always sleep with my
mouth open. I know
because it's open when I
wake up.'

'Please don't make me a
joke. End the interview with
what I believe . . . I want to
be an artist, an actress with
integrity.'

'The trouble with censors is
they worry if a girl has a
cleavage. They ought to
worry if she hasn't any.'

'I am not interested in
money. I just want to be
wonderful.'

'I used to say to myself,
What the devil have you got
to be proud about, Marilyn
Monroe? And I'd answer,
Everything, everything.'

MARILYN'S HOROSCOPE

Marilyn Monroe is a fascinating example of the dual nature of a Gemini. On the one hand there was all her fun and sparkle; on the other, dark pools of despair which no one truly understood.

HER SPIRITUAL NATURE

Together with her Leo Ascendant, Neptune, Jupiter, Saturn, and the Moon combine to give Marilyn a dynamic, strong-willed, and highly focused personality, determined to achieve her aims, but finding difficulty in adapting to changing circumstances. Her bucket-shaped chart, with Saturn as the 'handle' in her 4th House, shows an individual of extreme personal, but unconscious, force. All conscious influences need to be concentrated on counterbalancing the Saturn energy. However, because of its unconscious placement, and its square to Neptune, the Moon, and Jupiter, this energy will incline Marilyn to deep bouts of depression, loneliness and identity crises. Neptune (ruler of her 8th House) in the 1st House reinforces this quality of being driven by unconscious forces, while Pluto in Cancer, ruler of her 4th, adds a fated dimension to her life.

Against this introspective side is balanced a restless, extroverted personality. The Sun, Mercury, Moon, and Jupiter are all in Air signs; she will need to feel free to express herself creatively. Neptune in Leo in beautiful aspect to her Venus and the Moon-Jupiter partnership in Aquarius points to an irrepressible romantic idealism and a generous, humanitarian spirit. Lack of Earth, though (except for her Taurus Midheaven: the area of a chart most directed toward the outer world), won't make it easy for these qualities to find a practical, purposeful outlet.

MENTAL CHARACTERISTICS

The Sun and Mercury in Gemini indicate a positive mental outlook: quick, witty, educable and enquiring. Their position in the 10th House also adds a calculating shrewdness, and a desire to be taken seriously. However, these characteristics are close to the surface of her personality. Deep down, Saturn – with its challenging aspects to Neptune, the Ascendant, Jupiter, and the Moon (a formation known as a 'T-square') – shows a tendency for her mental faculties to be undermined by powerful emotional responses, leading to great mental stress and a difficulty in discriminating between the ideal and the real. (Sun in Gemini symbolizes ambiguity about self-identity.)

EMOTIONAL FACTORS

Her emotional nature is very strongly marked, especially as Saturn in Scorpio in the unconscious 4th House signifies deeply felt, repressed emotions about her psychological foundations. The interaction of Saturn in the 'T-square' with Neptune, Jupiter and the Moon represents feelings of guilt, loneliness, paranoia, hypersensitivity, and low self-esteem constantly battling for attention and release, yet at the same time challenged by emotional inhibition. Also, Pluto, Mars, and Saturn make a connection in the water signs of Cancer, Scorpio, and Pisces to indicate that her emotional response will be wild and irrational; the Moon opposing her Ascendant will intensify her moody and over-reactive tendencies.

Frequent identity-crises are likely through her 'T-square' and Sun-Gemini. Neptune in her 1st is associated with flight from emotional torment through drugs/alcohol. Yet, she has the benefit of a favorable aspect from Saturn to Mars and Uranus, bestowing a strong survival instinct and ability to endure hardship.

CHILDHOOD/FORMATIVE YEARS

Here we come to the crux of the chart. Saturn's placement in Scorpio often corresponds to a severely afflicted childhood, both materially and psychologically. The key issue here is the very frail, potentially unstable grasp of 'self' in the chart. The stressful aspect between Marilyn's Saturn and Neptune Ascendant in Leo will register in her childhood as a constant need to be coaxed, re-

assured, and given a sense of structure which establishes distinctive boundaries between 'self' and 'otherwise.'

The real danger for Marilyn is that the much evident 'T-square' has all the markings of the psychotic behavior common to a bulimic personality; the indiscriminately (Neptune) hungry ego (Leo Ascendant), desperate for nourishment (Moon-Jupiter) and deprived of essential nutrition (T-square to Saturn in Scorpio, 4th House), indulges in uncontrolled fantasy (Neptune) of self-glorification (Leo) which leads to rejection (Saturn square Moon) by self, or someone else, depression (Saturn square Jupiter) and a greater longing for the impossible (Moon-Jupiter opposite Saturn). And so the cycle spirals. . . . The protagonists in this psychodrama are, naturally, the parents, represented by the Sun (father) and the Moon (mother). If the aspects between and to these planets suggested positive familial influences, the outlook would be less dramatic, but they don't.

The father (Sun-Gemini in 10th) assumes an ambiguous role, probably through absence of some kind (literal, or psychological). As a result, Marilyn would have to develop her ability to survive through a profound sense of being abandoned, even though, on the surface, she might glamorize the father image. While she may pour her ambition into her 10th House career, and be successful, the lack of a support system represented by the father's 'absence' would place extremely serious limitations on her development into adulthood.

Quite simply, the emotional integration of the father principle – the male within her and therefore, in due course, men in general – is sorely missing. The crises of confidence this could be expected to trigger in her later life have been evaluated elsewhere in her relationships with men and her obsession with public recognition.

On the maternal side, the Saturn square to the Moon is the classic aspect signifying rejection by the mother. It may be that the mother, for whatever reason, is actually inattentive or unloving, or that the child simply selects to perceive her this way, but it is the perception that matters. And in this chart, the natural disposition of the 'T-square' to hypersensitivity, depression, emotional and mental instability – even paranoia – all interreact with the psychological estrangement from the mother. This deep-seated inferiority complex, channeled as it is through Saturn, is probably unconscious and therefore extremely difficult to counterbalance without professional help. Not only that, but the Saturn-Moon square in a woman's chart refers to her own femininity and consequently resentment of herself as a woman. The need to be mothered is a quality that she would carry into adulthood and particularly her relationships with men and her public.

TYPE OF CAREER

Marilyn's career would, without a doubt, be artistic: Venus in Aries close to her Taurus Midheaven highlights abundant creative talent. The prominence of her Neptune (ruler of cinema and photography) in Leo (theater, drama) and her Venus indicate a need for glamour, self-glorification, and mass-appeal; the Sun and Mercury in 10th House Gemini, a need to communicate. Saturn rules her house of work, so she will find routine work very restrictive and trouble with her employers is likely. Her career will certainly be vocational: interest in theater, cinema-work, photography, music, mysticism, and poetry are all strongly marked.

SUCCESS IN LIFE

Several factors point to a high level of achievement in her working life. Firstly, through Pluto's contact with the Moon's North Node, there is a fated quality about her career, with a consuming urge for public recognition and reaching out to the mass public. With the placements of her Sun, Mars, and Pluto, she will bring tremendous industry, self-will, some might say ruthlessness, into the pursuit of her career, demonstrating a single-mindedness of purpose not usually associated with a Gemini.

Secondly, the fortunate aspects between her Sun, Ascendant,

Jupiter, and Venus are powerful auguries of great popularity, fortunate contacts and the ability to project charm and a magnetic personality. The prominence of Venus, and its aspects generally, promises successful projection of physical beauty and sensuality through her public persona.

DESTABILIZING INFLUENCES

'Success' may come plentifully, but the dissolving nature of her Neptune contacts means her reaction to it will be ambivalent and at times plainly muddled. Both Saturn and her Sun will sharpen her ambition to be taken seriously in her career, thereby tempering any tendency to over-inflate her accomplishments. Sadly, Uranus brings a highly disruptive energy to her working life and relationships. She will be unreliable, emotionally volatile, highly strung, and extremely sensitive about her abilities. Furthermore, Pluto's contribution will probably ensure that there will be times when her work is seriously undermined by emotional crises in her life.

Fame will in all likelihood bring notoriety in the form of public scandal: Neptune in Leo opposite Jupiter and Venus in her 9th House, signify scandal and mass-media attention.

Initial decisions about career would be made, possibly, in her early teens, with a real turning point between 1946 and 1948 when a radical transformation of her personal image is indicated (Pluto crossing her Ascendant). At the age of 25/26, Jupiter passing over Marilyn's Venus-Midheaven inaugurates a phase of tremendous public triumph.

LOVE AND MARRIAGE

The area of Marilyn's life concerned with relationships is dominated by the Neptune-Jupiter polarity. Essentially this leads her to confuse love and friendship, which is further compounded by the influences of Uranus and Venus, drawing her to sudden, magnetic attractions and many compulsive affairs. Also Mars in Pisces in her 8th House leaves her highly impressionable nature (and almost childlike reliance on her would-be partner) vulnerable to seduction and deception.

Saturn, again, extends his cold hand to this side of her life. His difficult aspects to the Moon and Jupiter will drive Marilyn to yearn for love, but feel discontented once a relationship has become formalized. She will carry into her love-life the confusion, high emotional tension, and disintegration symptomatic of the 'T-square.' Divorce is probable (Uranus rules her 7th), as is infidelity out of a constant need to shore up her frail self-esteem.

Generally, she will not find it easy to balance her need to be dependent on others and to be desired with her yearning to be a free spirit. Her romantic nature will drive her relentlessly to seek the ideal partner (older men preferred).

There is a parallel here between her need for personal love and for public adoration. The same paradox is at work; an almost nymphomaniacal desire for public acclaim which is constantly undermined by her dread of being submerged by her 'screen goddess' image. As with her men, the problem for Marilyn is how to distinguish the celluloid personality that evolves from her affair with her public from who she really is. In both cases, it is this lack of ability to discriminate, exacerbated by a terror of being alone, which serves to disintegrate further her grasp on reality.

Her difficult love-life is also underpinned by Pluto and the Moon's North Node which point to powerful, even secret, lovers by which she is ultimately undone – adding a tragic twist to this area of her life. Her love-life will also be subject to scandal-mongers (Neptune in the 1st opposing Jupiter), especially its seamier side. In addition, there are indications of a traumatic sexual experience, such as rape, in her thirteenth year.

SEXUALITY

The position of her Mars and the sparkling aspect between Venus in Aries and Jupiter, would ordinarily imply a strongly marked sexual energy springing from a passionate, affectionate, and emotional nature. But Mars is weakly placed in Pisces and her interest in sex may come less from powerful drives than from a Neptunian longing to call a truce on the struggle for her individuality and to 'become one with everything.' The trouble is that this release is only reached if one is at ease with one's self-image and the auguries in this chart do not reveal that at all. As the emotions are likely to be severely inhibited, the release that a balanced sexuality could provide might be sought more readily through drug and/or alcohol abuse. Despite the prospect of many affairs and her strongly projected and magnetic sex appeal, she will have trouble discovering her sexuality, let alone expressing it. That does not mean she will recoil from sex; rather that she will be drawn more by the poetic fantasy in being desired than the act itself.

HEALTH

A poorly aspected Saturn, ruler of the 6th, indicates afflicted health: psychosomatic illnesses and vulnerable nervous system (Saturn square Neptune); gynecological problems, breasts, periods, water retention (Saturn square to Moon); liver, pituitary gland, swollen ankles (Saturn square to Jupiter); reproductive organs (Scorpio 4th House); anything limiting movement, such as rheumatism, arthritis etc (Capricorn 6th House).

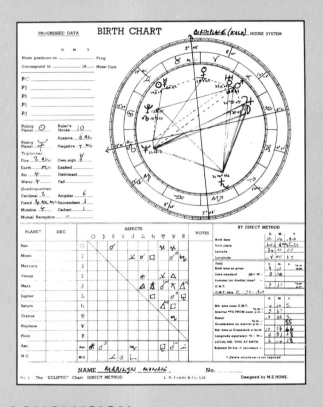

IN CONCLUSION

It has emerged that there is a fated quality to Marilyn's chart, both in her magnetism and in her pathos. To a large extent, the force behind this is Pluto in Cancer – in her 11th House – joining forces with the Moon's North Node in her 12th. Pluto moved into Cancer in 1913/14 and stayed there until 1937/38.

Pluto's aspect to the Moon's North Node has karmic undercurrents, intimating a destiny shaped by a heredity with the power to overwhelm her. Those who believe she committed suicide might argue that it did.

Interestingly, when she died her progressed Sun was overhead her natal Pluto, ruler of her 4th House, which denotes endings. Pluto destroys in order to transform; and with the progressed Sun this could be interpreted as Marilyn's own light being extinguished in order to be born again, phoenix-like, as a legend. For the conspiracy theorists, Uranus in her 8th House represents a peculiar death. As Pluto's position and contact with the Moon's North Node denotes clandestine involvements with powerful political figures, this might satisfy those who hold that her liaison with the Kennedys threatened to become a political embarrassment and led to her precipitate demise.

In a fashion typical of the Geminian duality, Marilyn's life was split between a uniquely glamorous projection of her talents and a deeply disturbed personality. With hindsight, it is tempting to read elements of a Greek tragedy into her life: a fatally flawed temperament finally over-reaching itself.

Felix Lyle

'In Hollywood a girl's virtue is much less important than her hairdo. You're judged by how you look, not by how you are. Hollywood's a place where they'll pay you a thousand dollars for a kiss, and fifty cents for your soul. I know, because I turned down the first offer often enough and held out for the fifty cents.'

Marilyn Monroe

'Do you remember when Marilyn Monroe died? Everybody stopped work, and you could see all that day the same expression on their faces, the same thought: How can a girl with success, fame, youth, money, beauty . . . how could she kill herself? Nobody could understand it because those are the things that everybody wants and they can't believe that life wasn't important to Marilyn Monroe, or that her life was elsewhere.'

Marlon Brando

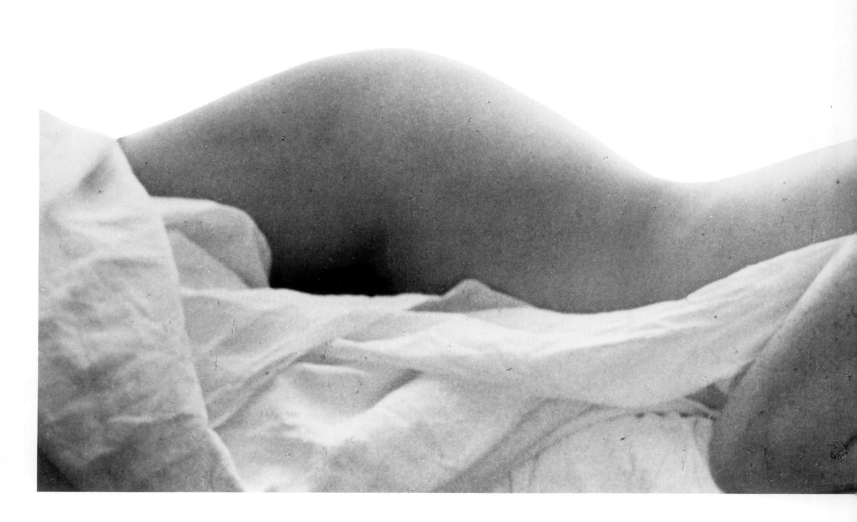

Left and below: *The photographs on these pages come from the session Bert Stern did late in June 1962 that was originally commissioned for* Vogue *magazine. Stern subsequently published them in his own book called* The Last Sitting.

Index & Acknowledgments

Figures in *italics* refer to illustrations.

ACKNOWLEDGMENTS

The author and publishers would like to thank Ran Barnes for designing the book, astrologer Felix Lyle for Marilyn's horoscope and Pat Coward for compiling the index. Photographic material was provided by the following agencies:

Ampas, pages: 32, 44, 45, 71, 76(bottom), 87, 90.
Bettman Archive, pages: 8(bottom), 18, 27(bottom), 57, 62-63, 64, 70, 96.
Camera Press, pages: 10, 14, 15, 17, 22, 39, 40, 60, 61(top), 68, 78, 80(top), 81, 83(both), 85(bottom), 86(top), 103, 111(both), 112-113, 116-117(all 4).
Joel Finler Collection, pages: 23, 43, 47, 76(top), 85(top).
Hulton Picture Company, page: 74.
Robert Hunt Library, pages: 69(bottom), 94(bottom), 106.
Kobal Collection, pages: 5, 9, 21(bottom), 26, 36, 38, 95.
Keystone, pages: 1, 19, 24, 27(top), 52, 75, 77(bottom), 88, 92, 93, 107, 110.
National Film Archive, London, pages: 25, 30(both), 41, 50, 51(top), 53(bottom), 54, 77(top), 82, 91(bottom), 94(top).
Topham Picture Library, pages: 16(bottom), 20, 58, 65, 66, 73(top), 79, 91(top).
Bob Willoughby, page: 105(top).
George Zeno Collection, pages: 2-3, 6. 8(top), 11, 12(both), 13, 16, 21(top), 28, 31, 33, 34, 35, 37, 42, 46, 48, 49, 51(bottom), 53(top), 55, 59, 61(bottom), 69(top), 72, 73(bottom), 80(bottom), 84, 86(bottom), 97-99, 104, 105(bottom).